MAGIC BOOMERANG

Frané Lessac and Mark Greenwood

Plantagenet Press

FREMANTLE

First published 1994 by
PLANTAGENET PRESS PTY LTD
PO Box 934, Fremantle, Western Australia 6160.
Telephone: (619) 430 44 66   Facsimile: (619) 430 5217

Reprinted 1995

Consultant: Mandy Corunna, Yirra Yaakin Youth Theatre.

Typeset in Bookman

ISBN 0 646 17790 7

For our parents and our children

Frané & Mark

A magic adventure began
on this day,
with a gift in the post from far,
far, away.
Uncle Max from Australia,
Kalgoorlie in fact,
had posted a present so
carefully wrapped.

"Greetings Dear Cody," the letter began,

"I hope you have fun with this old boomerang.

It has amazing powers so legends here say.

It will always come back if you throw it away."

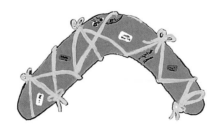

Cody ran to the park and looked up to the sky,
threw the old boomerang and it started to fly.
It spun round and round and began to come back.
As he reached out to catch it, his head got a whack!

Soon Cody woke up in a very
strange land,
he gazed all around and tried hard
to stand.
Gum trees were swaying in a warm
summer breeze,
wildflowers bloomed in the shade of
the trees;
Sturt pea, wattle, coolabah
and more,
banksia, bottlebrush and
kangaroo paw.

Suddenly Cody heard a rustling sound,

a tap on his shoulder made him turn around.

"My name is Napuru, you are not alone,

I'll show you Australia, this land is our home.

This boomerang has magic," Napuru explained.

"It can carry us far over any terrain."

"If we dream of a place and both close our eyes,
we can go anywhere the old boomerang flies."
So they dreamt of a spot in the outback somewhere,
where the animals played and soon they were there.

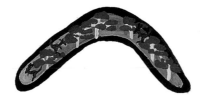

They sat by a billabong and there in the shade,

kangaroos, koalas and wombats played.

In a clear shallow stream a platypus swam,

in the distance emus and dingos ran.

Kookaburras laughed but the cockatoos knew,

if the boys made a wish their dreams would come true.

The boomerang was thrown and the boys made a wish,
to escape from the heat and swim with the fish.
Into sparkling blue waters they both splashed and dived
at the Great Barrier Reef, where the wobbegongs hide.
They swam with striped tigersharks, parrot fish too
and large coral trout with spots sapphire blue,
a small school of sweetlips, angelfish and more.
They saw crabs and stingray on the dark ocean floor.

Again the old boomerang soared
into the skies
and just as the boys were opening
their eyes,
raindrops were falling!
It was humid and hot!
A tropical forest, believe it or not!
Dainty green tree frogs hopped
into a pond,
waterfalls splashed on the
rocks beyond.
Frangipani and jasmine smelt
wonderfully sweet,
pawpaw and jackfruit were
delicious to eat!

For the Northern Territory the boys set out next,

to a deep muddy river where the crocodiles rest.

They sat on a log and peered underneath,

Napuru shouted, "This log has got teeth!"

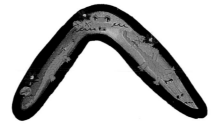

Cody threw the boomerang

and took Napuru's hand.

They ran so quickly,

they hardly touched sand.

Napuru said, breathless,

"There's the desert to see.

Uluru at sunset is the place to be."

As the friends gazed in wonder at
this sacred site,
the sun set to the west and day turned
to night.
Aboriginal people danced, played
and sang a dreamtime tale
of a magic boomerang.
The moon high above was glowing
so bright
and the Southern Cross twinkled in
the dark night.
Cody lay down by a warm glowing fire,
tiny sparks flickered,
he began to tire.

He gazed at the sky and started to dream

of his friend Napuru and the places they'd seen.

Suddenly Cody woke up. He was back in the park!

With the old boomerang he ran home before dark.

What a magic adventure he'd had on that day,

with a gift in the post from far, far away.

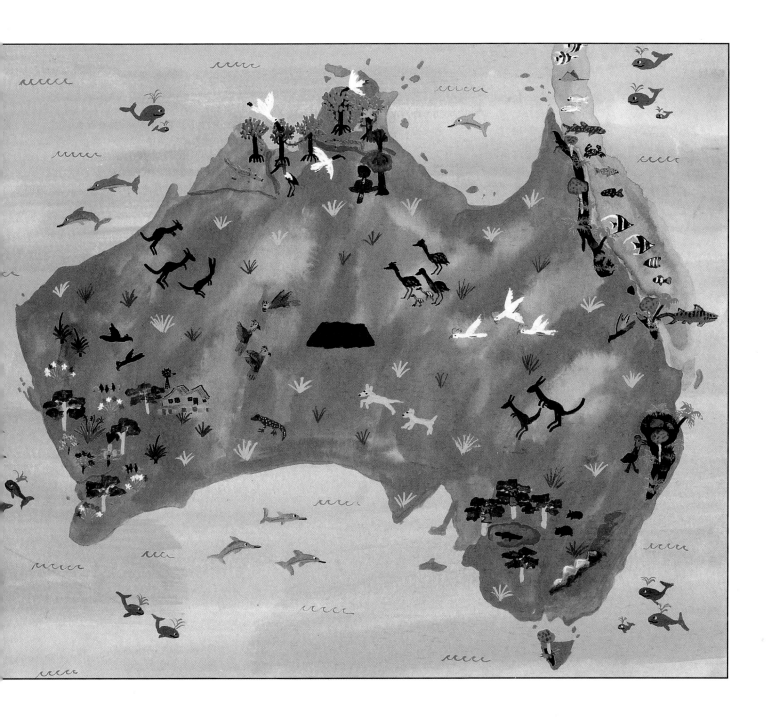

Frané Lessac has illustrated several popular children's books. Her books offer an insight into a range of cultures and have been translated into various languages. Frané's paintings have been exhibited in galleries throughout the world, including England, France, the United States, the Caribbean and Australia. After spending some years in the Caribbean she now lives in Fremantle with her family.

Mark Greenwood has contributed to two Caribbean titles illustrated by Frané Lessac. Magic Boomerang is his first Australian title. Mark is a successful musician and has spent many years in the United States and England recording and performing. He is now based in Fremantle where he lives with his wife and two children.

Special thanks to:
Joanne Hallis, Alma Toomath, Lynda and Bernie Ryder,
Gail Brandon-Stewart and of course, Roger, Trish and Angela.

Frané & Mark

Other titles from Plantagenet Press

Off Like Flies
'Til She Dropped Her Strides
Chook On Sundays
Land's Edge

Future Titles

Nullarbor
Outback Christmas